PowerPhonics™

On My Sled

Learning the SL Sound

Colleen Adams

The Rosen Publishing Group's
PowerKids Press™
New York

I get out my sled in the winter.

I slide in the snow on my sled.

I slide down a hill on my sled.

My mom pulls my sled up
the hill.

I can slide fast on my sled.

I can go slow on my sled.

I sled by a girl on skates.

I sled by a boy who slips
and slides.

We slip and slide in the snow.

It is fun to slide on a sled!

Word List

sled

slide

slip

slow

Instructional Guide

Note to Instructors:
One of the essential skills that enable a young child to read is the ability to associate letter-sound symbols and blend these sounds to form words. Phonics instruction can teach children a system that will help them decode unfamiliar words and, in turn, enhance their word-recognition skills. We offer a phonics-based series of books that are easy to read and understand. Each book pairs words and pictures that reinforce specific phonetic sounds in a logical sequence. Topics are based on curriculum goals appropriate for early readers in the areas of science, social studies, and health.

Letter/Sound: **sl** – Write the words *sip* and *lip*. Have the child decode the words and underline the parts that are alike. Write *slip*. Remind the child that they must blend consonants **s** and **l** in order to decode the word.
- Pronounce the following words: *slide – sip – slow*. Have the child name the two words that start with **sl**. Continue with: *slip – sled – said, slate – sleep – sun, slap – sad – slam*, etc. List the child's responses and have them underline **sl** in each of the words.

Phonics Activities: Write different word endings on a chalkboard or dry-erase board, such as *eep, ed, ide, ip*. Add **sl** to each of these to make a word. Assist the child with reading the words and using them in sentences.
- Ask the child to think of words that rhyme with each **sl** word by changing the beginning consonant sounds.
- Have the child find all the **sl** words in the text. Assist them with writing a story about a snowy day using these words and other **sl** words to describe winter activities (*slushy, slippery, slope, sleet*, etc.).
- Review the blends (such as **bl**, **pl**, **gl**, **cl**) that the child has learned from previous lessons. Write a story about a snowy day. Ask the child to supply a suitable word beginning with the indicated consonant blend. (Example: *One snowy day, Pat called the kids who lived on his **bl** [block]. He said, "Come outside and **pl** [play]." Pat put on warm **cl** [clothes] and boots. He was **gl** [glad] to **pl** [play] in the snow.*)

Additional Resources:
- Burke, Jennifer S. *Cold Days.* Danbury, CT: Children's Press, 2000.
- Hader, Berta. *The Big Snow.* New York: Simon & Schuster Children's, 1993.
- Schaefer, Lola M. *Cold Day.* Mankato, MN: Capstone Press, Inc., 2000.

Published in 2002 by The Rosen Publishing Group, Inc.
29 East 21st Street, New York, NY 10010

Book Design: Haley Wilson

Photo Credits: Cover, p. 7 © Sandra Stambaugh/Index Stock; pp. 3, 5 © Eric Fowke/Index Stock; p. 9 © Lawrence Sawyer/Index Stock; p. 11 © Table Mesa Prod./Index Stock; p. 13 © Scott Barrow/International Stock; p. 15 © Nancy Sheehan/Index Stock; p. 17 © Gary Hubbell/Index Stock; p. 19 © Benelux Press/Index Stock; p. 21 © Mark Gibson/Index Stock.

Library of Congress Cataloging-in-Publication Data

Adams, Colleen.
 On my sled : learning the SL sound / Colleen Adams.—1st ed.
    p. cm. — (Power phonics/phonics for the real world)
  ISBN 0-8239-5952-X (lib. bdg.)
  ISBN 0-8239-8297-1 (pbk.)
  6 pack ISBN 0-8239-9265-9
  1. Sledding—Juvenile literature. [1. Sledding   2. English
  language—Consonants] I. Title. II. Series.
  GV856 .A36 2001
  796. 9' 5—dc21
                                    2001-1055

Manufactured in the United States of America